The Happier Life

by the same author

TERRY STREET

The Happier Life

DOUGLAS DUNN

FABER & FABER
3 Queen Square, London

First published in 1972
by Faber and Faber Limited
3 Queen Square London WC1
Printed in Great Britain by
Latimer Trend & Co Ltd Plymouth

ISBN 0 571 09931 9

For my father and mother

Acknowledgements

Some of these poems have already appeared in
the following periodicals: *Antæus*; *Encounter*; *The London
Magazine*; *New Statesman*; *Phoenix*; the *Review*;
Spectator; *Stand*; *Times Literary Supplement*; and
some also appeared as a pamphlet collection—
Backwaters—published as a supplement to the
Review, No. 25, Spring 1971.

'Nights of Sirius' appeared originally in *The
New Yorker*.

'Night' was first published by the Poem of
the Month Club.

Contents

The Garden

Neighbours hate it, and know us by it.
We do not mind at all. We rather like it.
For gardens need nothing specially
And tall weeds are better weeds,

And the dandelions, my toy streetlamps,
Are far too personally involved with me
To tolerate digging and other mischief.
Frog and shrew, and the cat's concubines

Are at home here. Short grass is their enemy.
So I'm sure they love me. They don't object
To my running the broken lawnmower
Over the daisies; they know I'm just clearing

A space for the deckchair. Dog's mercury
And bramble please them enough, and me too.
Green's green, here as on any pampered lawn
Where whispering sprinklers make plaster statues

Of mock Phidias weep, the ruins of classicism.
And here the wave shapes of the wild thorn
Are as angry as cultured brothers growing
In a ground nervous with learned tending.

Milieu for rare butterflies, as well as friends
Lunching in a miniature glade, something fresh
Might happen here, unworked and gladdening.
Shoots of young sycamore, dock and thistle,

These are part of this unflowering iconoclasm,
Green and recurrent, smelling of dust and rain.
Other gardens smell of perfumed arrangements
Like tarts' bedrooms, pilfered by bumble-bees

And angry woollies, like these little girls
Searching for coquettish accessories
Or petals to mash in a jam jar with soap
And vinegar, making, they say, cat's medicine.

Wallflower soup's an unwelcome new taste sensation,
And a cat with a rose in its ear looks very silly.
These furtive pets escape into our garden,
To happy sleep in convolvulus-shredded shades.

They must look up to us. At least, they ought to,
For we need allies crusading our grassy way
Through Ted Heath's Britain, and animal friendships
Might add beguiling eccentricity

To this oppositional horticulture
That upsets, the neighbours say, all their decent
Trimmings. 'Why not *do* something?' But this,
Like the *hortus mentis*, is not so untended.

Here we are perfect. Metaphysical greenbirds
Perch over sunlit leaves; our feet converse
With the refreshing grass. And here I am
A very old man of twenty-eight, glad

Of this random perfection, and you, so still
We are as islands on an island, everything
Ebbing into green around us; we know
Though this might look neglected, it might grow.

The River Through the City

The river of coloured lights, black stuff
The tired city rests its jewels on.
Bad carnival, men and women
Drown themselves under the bridges.
Death-splash, and after, the river wears
The neon flowers of suicides.
Prints of silence ripple where they went in.
An old man rows a black boat and slides past
Unnoticed, a god in an oilskin coat.
He feeds the uncatchable black fish.
They know where Hitler is hiding.
They know the secrets behind sordid events
In Central Europe, in America and Asia,
And who is doing what for money.
They keep files on petty thieves, spies,
Adulterers and their favourite bureaucrats.
That's one old man who's nobody's uncle.
That's one fish you don't want with your chips.
Iron doors bang shut in the sewers.

The Friendship of Young Poets

There must have been more than just one of us,
But we never met. Each kept in his world of loss
The promise of literary days, the friendship
Of poets, mysterious, that sharing of books
And talking in whispers in crowded bars
Suspicious enough to be taken for love.

We never met. My youth was as private
As the bank at midnight, and in its safety
No talking behind backs, no one alike enough
To be pretentious with and quote lines at.

There is a boat on the river now, and
Two young men, one rowing, one reading aloud.
Their shirt sleeves fill with wind, and from the oars
Drop scales of perfect river like melting glass.

Nights of Sirius

Unknown men tonight will put
One last hand to a life's work,
Hobbyhorse or a pedantic search
For private seriousness;
Or add a wise last paragraph
To the privately published
Volume of family history,
Put back on the cherished shelf
Of an eccentric library
To be read in ten years' time
By a bookish grandson.

High summer, and dog-star nights
Are still and hot, accepting death
And notebooks, snapshot albums,
Treasured books and objects,
A chair, his favourite tie—
Possessions the dead have left,
What pleased them, passed their time,
And shall, like wives, preserve
Their marks of ownership,
Ways of what it felt like to be theirs,
Touch, pulse, the smell of hands.

At a Yorkshire Bus-stop

Little girls with dog-eared jotters,
The plumber's and the barman's daughters,
Skip round the bus-stop.—Ankle socks
And polished shoes and home-made frocks,
Initialed hanky in a cuff
And mittens lined with furry stuff.
Somebody's cleaning woman looks
At maps and open picture books
In the travel agent's window.
Where will she go, where will she go,
Madrid by BEA, by rail
To Istanbul with mop and pail?
Or outdo Madam with a rest
At Marrakesh or Bucharest?
　　The bus is late, my Number Ten
With girls to school and back again;
With the unmotorized to jobs,
Blind men to visit friends, and slobs
Who've had their licenses withheld
For driving sloshed, a lamp-post felled,
Or on a zebra-crossing struck
A boy sent shopping out of luck.
And the untaxied mourners come
To the crematorium,
Or high-class ladies on their way
To coffee mornings, or to play
Bridge or adultery. These noons
Of bus-queues and four-door saloons
Passing each other! Going places,
Slow housewives with worried faces,

Older than I am, nothing to do
With what the young like or what's new;
And lady artists in a *Minor*
Off to paint where light is finer;
The leggy keep-fit typists' bikes,
Executives bewailing strikes;
The overladen shopping matrons
And poodles barking in white Citroëns;
And students in the yellow vans
With passengers like partisans
From training camps deep in the Wolds;
The Lord Lieutenant in a Rolls.
    It's easy to astound with traction
When getting there's the Big Attraction
Of the age. The more horsepower,
Space in the back or miles per hour,
The bigger chance that The Ambition—
Sex in one stunning repetition—
Will be fulfilled. But I assert
Praise of the late and unalert,
And beat a drum and wave a banner
For those who never touch a spanner,
All my undriving friends in queues
Who cannot fix a gear or fuse,
And those who shout in traffic jams
That others cause: 'Bring back the trams!'
In ages fast or instamatic
Most poets will defend the static.
But though it is original
To praise the shy or virginal
At any time, my friends insist
I give my praise this added twist:
Although with cars they have no truck
That doesn't mean they cannot fuck.
    Not much really happens when

I'm waiting for the Number Ten,
Time inactively domestic
Spent in bus-queues watching traffic,
And noticing that men I know
Drive past without a wave or show
Of recognition. Wasting time's
A way of finding out time's
Unimportant. One day there passed
A creaking relic of the past,
A dozen workmen with a cart.
Robust dead age, that moved my heart
To beauties of the obsolete,
The heavy crunch of booted feet
Where wheels should be, pedestrian,
Heroic, almost Grecian,
Like fresh supplies for Syracuse
Dragged up by Sicanus before queues
In sunlight tinged with petrol fumes.
Time re-enacts and then resumes.
Then fled back to the measured praise
Unwithered in Thucydides
That glimpse of legendary days,
As if dissolved back into time
Not much like this, no tick or chime
Or scientific pendulum
To regulate when buses come
And take away the massed breadwinners
To television sets and dinners.
    Again I watched the Fast and Slow
Enact their licensed rodeo
Of aluminium and chrome
Tame instruments that take them home.
And all the city's destinations,
Shops and homes and railway stations,
Each place of work, the park and zoo,

Were asking I be taken too:
To hives of the unvisited
And places where they put the dead,
On one perpetual round to meet
The thin, the pregnant and replete,
The half-asleep, the cross and nosey,
The till and trigger virtuosi,
Those deep in shit and those in clover,
The astute and the funny-all-over.
I watched, and all my feelings dried.
'But sympathy has limits,' cried
My miserable Mrs. Mop,
The girls and old men at the stop,
And women in the butcher's shop.
How could they know, though by my side,
I'm going nowhere for the ride,
All my life inside a bus
From terminus to terminus
With many others. It's a miracle
A bus could be so bloody lyrical,
The latest breed of underdog
In counties underneath the fog.

The Musical Orchard

Girls on mopeds rode to Fécamp parties,
And as they passed the ripened orchard
Cheered an old man's music,
Not knowing it was sad.
Those French tunes on the saxophone,
The music inside fruit!

Backwaters

They are silent places, dilapidated cities
Obscure to the nation, their names spoken of
In the capital with distinct pejorative overtones.

For some, places mean coming to or going from,
Comedians and singers with their suitcases
Packed with signed photographs of themselves;

Business-men in sharp suits, come to buy and sell,
Still seeking their paradise of transactions,
The bottomless market, where the mugs live.

For others, places are sites for existence,
Where roads slow down and come to a stop
Outside where it's good to be, particular places

Where instantly recognized people live,
The buses are a familiar colour and life is
Utterly civilian, all uniforms

Merely the kind insignia of postmen
And meter readers. There complacency means
Men are almost the same, and almost right.

And for a few, places are only the dumps
They end up in, backwaters, silent places,
The cheapest rooms of the cheapest towns.

These darker streets, like the bad days in our lives,
Are where the stutterers hide, the ugly and clubfooted,
The radically nervous who are hurt by crowds.

They love the sunlight at street corners
And the tough young men walking out of it,
And the police patrol. Poverty makes fools of them.

They have done so little they are hardly aware of themselves.
Unmissed, pensioned, at the far end of all achievements,
In their kiln-baked rooms, they are permanent.

Leisure No End

Idleness is the great attraction, clothes,
Music, an appearance. Some call that love.
Freckled daughters of the country Irish
Come here to find it, and find themselves instead
Hardworked by protestants in drab hotel rooms.
Essentially rural whores, essentially innocent,
They are looking for nothing to do,
A life of soft hands and refreshing baths,
High-spirited nights in a plush apartment.
Their futures are only personal,
Nothing to do with us. Ten pounds might buy
One hour of their lives, insanitary farms,
The dishonoured fathers they cannot love,
A battered gramophone and a confirmation dress.

This Year and Next

December thirty-first drags next year in
Like tractors with a heavy gun.

Still there, grazing near the fences,
Herds of armoured divisions;

Big boots on the European snowdrops,
Tarts of all fashions in the jumping shops.

Morning Bedroom

The blue telephone has been near her mouth,
And clothes on the pink basketweave chair
Have touched her where it matters; and on her
Dressing-table brushes lie like sleeping pets.
        I have wasted my youth,
I have watched the bright clasp in her hair,
    Her lipstick's trace on cigarettes,
    A heap of crumpled underwear.

My pillow, you are a dead pig, a skin
Filled with last night and too much drink, the smell
Of our heads and our hair and stale perfume.
Her ear is one obese wing of a moth.
        This is how days begin.
When curtains and the sunlight tremble,
    She wakes, the room takes shape, and both
    Together in the morning bedroom,

My head already on the verge of ache
And she already buoyant, yawning, fit,
Look to the daytime having lived the night.
She rings the little bell and breakfast comes
        With fuss that flunkies make
To keep life easy. We eat, and sunlit
    Windows flame with red geraniums
    The bedroom of the sybarite.

I kiss her as I would my own reflection,
With disgust, carelessness of disapproval,
Then turn my head away, as if lips cut

On hers, a stranger's flesh not met before.
　　　I know her well. Her son,
She says, to make our trick obscene. But all
　　Love is like the love of the whore,
　　No holds are barred and no doors shut.

She taught me how to be in love that is
But is not love, shallow-kiss, nothing-touch,
All dainty treacheries of lust disguised
By stylish words and fashionable clothes.
　　　The brothel of a kiss!
Inside her mouth fly fixtures of the hutch,
　　Towels, basin, chocolates, rose,
　　The smell of sweat deodorized.

All that, I've drawn in, and I've become like her,
Kept for what boyishness she's left to me.
Inseparable, we walk at noon, and eat
In town, amused to hear what people say
　　　Wherever we enter:
Knowing smiles, and whispers, 'What age is she?'
　　We stroll then to a small café
　　And settle down to watch the street

Through little peep-holes in the steamed-up glass,
Our favourite game. The likely girls tilt by,
Arrived from the unsatisfying provinces;
A couple overstayed from lunch rush back
　　　To work. Policemen pass,
The city sweeps to the mortality
　　Of afternoons. The drinking pack,
　　Over-laden from off-licenses,

Skid on our glass and look in through the smudge.
She phones the car then leaves the Greek a tip

He won't forget. Home, to the quiet square
And servants, salves and Pernod by the pool
    And then a half-hour trudge
Through her ointmented flesh before our dip,
  A lazy swim in the azure
  Heat, float on transparent wool.

Night's dinner, I'm nibbled by the shine
The silver plates wink when servants put them down.
Who wonders where I am? I'm lost. She ties
Me here by occult riggishness, my will's
    Subdued, no longer mine.
From the cheapest streets and cheapest rooms in town
  She picked me up with promises
  And groomed me in the riggish skills.

We double through maps of lubriciousness,
Turkish tonight, tomorrow night Chinese.
One woman Storeyville, your navy rides
At anchor in the perfumed sheets, to you
    I am the vast caress
Of all that's carnal, and I'm trained to please,
  Exclusive to your private stew.
  Freedom's rotted: Madame decides,

And what she says, I do. But I'm afraid.
Who came before, and if I go, who's next?
What happens to the cast-offs? Each day
I see a surly, silent rival gain
    More ground and wish me dead.
A year out of the world, who would be vexed
  If I shall not go home again?
  And yet I wither if I stay.

She's made me choose from life, something plain
But something else, alternative too big
To have a name, where bones break and breath
Expires, mugs sign contracts, nations treaties,
     The unlucky die in pain.
No bitch will trap me there, for here's one dog
    Who wants his life to end in death
    And live in peace and happiness.

First light, the beauty of the disenchantment,
When the saliva is thin, before I cough,
And tastes cake on my lips, I curse her with
My first and golden spit the morning after
     All night falling, stagnant
Sleep beside beside her. In her arms, white trough,
    She is grass and water, laughter;
    She is more than life, more than death.

I watch the room, the sunlight through red fibre
    Cast blood-like blossoms over her.
And from an empty bottle of rare scotch
Used in my courting as a vase, I watch
    A petal fall from last night's rose
    To land on scattered underclothes,
    And mime, in falling curves, that it,
    Rightful beauty, can live in dirt.

Supreme Death

Fishing on a wide river from a boat
A corpse was caught, her black hair like a huge weed,
The hook stuck in a black shroud strangely marked.

There were others. Hundreds gathered round the boat,
Some turning, their white faces like pillows.
I lost my oars, and the river quickened.

On the towpath, men in their hundreds
Ran with the tide, singing, and pushing,
When they felt like it, some poor fool into the river.

Death, the best of all mysteries, layer
After layer is peeled off your secrecy
Until all that is left is an inexplicable ooze.

Too late, it is myself.
Too late, my heart is a beautiful top.
Too late, all the dead in the river are my friends.

Celtica

The red-haired have the whitest skin,
Beauty of a wet climate. They should sit
Beside waterfalls, many miles from traffic
And Saxon eyes, reserved for that lover
Who sits among peaks, in the disguise
Of clouds and mist, stones and rain.
Where is the blood, the beginning?
A nation's beauty, like a flame
Lasting on charred wood, survives
In a few bodies as if true or pernicious.

The Boon Companions

I see you munch your nails, grazing across
Your fingertips, sometimes watching the door
For a favoured entrant, a third of us.
The pub enjoys our wait, and keeps the score
Of waitings watched by it. We are small loss
To its varnished eyes. But here we focus
Presence, we take up room, and standing still
Shape in our minds the face of the missing third,
Who talks too much, but does not keep his word.
There are places to be, where you talk, fill
Glasses, greet loudly, remembering old times
Exaggerated, inventing obscene rhymes.
You turn and say, '*He* does not understand,'
And raise your glass in your nibbled hand.

Night

Night, no one forgets you, or your several voices,
The laughter of lovers and quick dressing
Of adulterers, who put socks on inside out
In the darkness that favours divorce detectives,
The almost silent trees, and cries from sleep
That express the unutterable, the undisclosed.

Light for the furtive, too frequent not to be missed
By crooks or perfectionists, the saintly
At their long prayers, safe-breakers and lovers
At their intricate fingerings. Should this city
Burn tonight, it will be dark where I am,
All the absurd crimes of the night have found me here.

I will be among the ashes they rake about in
For the mayor's regalia, the bank's gold ingots.
The worst weeds growing in the desolation
Will grow from me, my powdery ash will choke
The throats of the prigs. The man is a liar
Who says he has not found my grey dirt in his heart.

Syndrome

When the present beach generation
Has lost its tan, and pushing pens
In the back room of the supermarket,
Putting up with that perpetual winter
Called gainful employment
By government and moneylenders,
It will be time to see what they stood for,
Weighing regret against pleasure.

When the rising young executives
Have risen, and their suits are being tailored
Just that little bit more behind the fashion
But much more expensively, and taking
Six weeks off instead of four
And going to Jamaica instead of Majorca,
It will be time to see what they stood for,
Weighing regret against pleasure.

Who will reach conclusions?
Only the beach boys and the power men
Past and present, taking the form
Of sadness and petulance. Both wasted,
Both neglected the best, and find themselves
Appearing in sermons by poet and clergyman.
What is the best? Not idleness, not careers.
The only answer is to live quietly, miles away.

C

Billie 'n' Me

You could never have been a friend of mine,
Even if I played as sweet as dead Lester
Three feet from you, because you mean too much,
Your voice opens all doors on fed-up love.

There were dreams of you, in the ideal night club,
The members gone, just you, the band, and me
In my white tuxedo resisting requests to leave,
Then walking back to my pampered hotel room

In a dawn of fanciful New York heights,
Wondering how you'd take my roses sent at noon,
The invitation to lunch, that you ignored,
The lyrics I had written but you would not sing,

Black, dead, put down by love that was too much,
Mismanaged pleasures. And silent now
As the saxophones in Harlem pawnshops,
Your voice that meant how tough love is.

Midweek Matinée

The lunch hour ends and men go back to work,
Plumbers with long bags, whistling office boys
With soup on their ties and pee on their shoes,
Typists with a sandwich and a warm coke.

The indolent or lucky are going to the cinema.
There too go the itinerant heavy drinkers,
Who take the piss out of bus conductors
Or fall asleep in public reading rooms

Over unlikely learned periodicals.
They come in late, just after closing time,
And sprawl in the cheap front seats
Dressed in the raincoats of a thousand wet nights,

Muttering with the lips of the unknown kisses.
Legendary, underserving drunks, beggarly
And good for pity or laughter, you show
What happens to men who are not good at life,

Where happiness is demanded and lives are lived
For entertainment. I watch you sleep,
Grey humps in an empty cinema. You're dangerous.
All wish you were not there, cramping the style.

You are very bad, you are worse than civilized,
Untouched by seriousness or possessions,
Treading the taxpayers' roads, being found
Incapable in public places, always hungry,

Totally unlike what people should be—washed,
Happy, occupied, idle only in snatches
Of paid-for amusement or cynical truancies.
You have cut yourself off from barbers and supermarkets.

I don't want you here on my page, pink faces
Under spit and stubble, as fools or martyrs.
You are not new, you have nothing to sell.
You are walking evictions. You have no rentbooks.

You never answer telephones or give parties.
If you have a sense of humour, I want to know.
You claim the right to be miserable
And I can't stand what you bring out into the open.

The Hull Sit-in

An old man leans upon a fence, his wife
Weighed down by shopping bags, while up the street
Three hundred students sit to make their mark
Too young in politics, the uncertain truths;
Lank and sinister, like handsome Deaths,
The menacing youths in the Admin Block.
Pathetic age, power comes to nothing;
The young are dying, the old are already dead.

Students of political history and sociology
Throng round the door of the institution,
Singing drivel without irony, and
Dressed as if to amuse old men, or else
Prolong the role of timeless motley.
The whip, sirrah, the whip.

The Hunched

They will not leave me, the lives of other people.
I wear them near my eyes like spectacles.
Sullen magnates, hunched into chins and overcoats
In the back seats of their large cars;
Scholars, so conscientious, as if to escape
The things too real, the names too easily read,
Preferring language stuffed with difficulties;
And the children, furtive with their own parts;
The lonely glutton in the sunlit corner
Of an empty Chinese restaurant;
The coughing woman, leaning on a wall,
Her wedding-ring finger in her son's cold hand,
In her back the invisible arch of death.
What makes them laugh, who lives with them?

I stooped to lace a shoe, and they all came back,
Mysterious people without names or faces,
Whose lives I guess about, whose dangers tease.
And not one of them has anything at all to do with me.

The Shirt

There is something strange about this shirt,
As if it had been a dead friend's
Who only now is being missed and understood,
And he has left it, hardly worn, for someone else
To wear. Death is all round me, bold and clean,
So white, orthodox and unacceptable.
This was my old shirt. It feels like wax now,
And I cannot bear to look at myself in it.
I should run away in this shirt, to where
It was worn, the white shadows of those
Who once were alive, the strangest company.
There is someone there the way I used to be.
Haunting the old roads, I've looked for him.
He always sees me coming and keeps away,
Running with fast shadows on the fair slopes.
I wear his shirt, death's shirt, legacy
I did not know of. His mother put it
Clean and crisp into a scented drawer.

Emblems

Rich nights in another climate—
White tables and the best Moselle,
A garden that slopes to a clear river;
Style I cannot make and was not born to claim.

And the factory is humming at full production
Just over the hill, making money,
Whispering, a big fish without eyes,
The most profound unhappiness.

The Sportsmen

Scum, they have fast cars and money
And take other men's wives to play tennis.

They are always with us, making us laugh
At parties, in the pub. They live for prowess,

To be good at pastimes. Their times will come.
An ordinary man will beat them at their favourite games,

They will be murdered in bedrooms,
Their cars pressed into squares of scrap.

The Happier Life

There are no pure. Some tried. They are dead now.
To be both wild and clean; I would allow
Myself that—excess of sex without shame,
A proper indulgence, harmlessly untame.
   What city could contain that, or permit
One happy life to make a fool of it?
Capitals were made for government and love,
The flag, fop's handkerchief and yellow glove;
Polemics in tall rooms, bright London troops,
Justice in the courts, bargains in the shops.
Authority is here, old and royal,
All books in English, all things available.
This city lives off Hull, Hell and Halifax,
All sad varieties of furtive sex
And irresistible beauties of shame or wealth,
Facilities of spirit to soothe them with.
Only the fittest endure the happiness
Of the capital, worse than it ever was,
The London of all indulgences, worth
Twice the stern propriety of the heavy North.
Both are equally unkind. Moderate
And better ways prosper only in private;
Men find their own and disaffiliate
From all repulsiveness that makes them hate.
Or should, rather than fight what makes them sick
With speeches of a stylised politic.
Wise apathy's a proper stance, aspiring
To wry complacencies of the retiring—
To villas by a lake, a silent farm,
Or any mortgaged hut away from harm.

And some go further; stimulated mind
Invents *Utopias*, and escapes to find
In bubbles of Arcadian alcohol
The townless slopes of standard pastoral
Glow like populated glass. Men and herds—
Not so easy. Only disaffected bards
Or eldest sons brought up to farm see red
When motorways and concrete meadows spread
Unproductive splendour of men's comforts
To stifle country walks and Ceres' efforts.
Society's a sham with many gods,
Immune to peace, contentedly at odds,
Fragmented into class and sheltered clique
That reason life by self-preserving pique,
Yet never quite forget man could unite
His blood and species, a cause the armies fight
To stop, orators lie, bad poets write.
  Community's a myth. We'll never find
The men whose happier lives and peace of mind
Outstay all changes, all rises in income,
Resisting the pretensions of the scum,
Who build the easeful place, where all is sound,
Where squares are squares and every circle's round,
A city where all needs are taken care of
By good men oozing with official love,
The houses comfy and the statutes lost,
A city of the mild and self-engrossed
Where super-marketeering is a crime
And business-men stay hidden all the time,
Their only job to sell the hidden vices
Men need to live, draught beer and almond ices.
And freshly minted coins sustain this peace,
One equal wage from Nowhere, got with ease
For tilling your own land, podding your peas,
A horse to plough with and a cow to milk,

And men known by their place—'Dunn, of that Ilk,'
So each man is his own aristocrat,
With wife, their sons and daughters, dog and cat.
Each coin's embossed with spade and woolly peach,
The labour and its fruit, and same for each.
The till and trigger virtuosi rot
In distant mausoleums; glory's not
A welcome target here; no one gives thanks
For advertising or for heavy tanks.
On the unpolluted, unmanœuvred field
The mowers mow and lovers love, to yield
Effortless children, grain that flows like mirth,
And both are harvest of the managed earth,
The happier life, the uncompetitive.
　　Yet even there men shake the wretched sieve
And sift through life to find right ways to live,
Listening to the boulevard philosophers
Describe a *better* life, one the elders
Suppress, they say. So secret enclaves scheme
To bring to life a dream within the dream.
　　Mistakes, disaster, rotten circumstance
Unpopulate the landscapes of Romance;
Unmoral and unmanned, thus simplified
Back into fern and foxglove spades denied
Much chance to grow, the wolf comes back to stalk
The paths that brave new settlers might walk;
The land thus wild, eft and dispas, stoat and snake,
Prowl in the wild wheat, inhabit the brake
Of maddened bramble barbing every trail
That once had brought men visitors and mail.
A land, they thought, that all wild beasts had fled.
But they came back before they'd burned the dead,
The ravished women, disappointed men,
Butchered children, each last Arcadian,
And went as slaves back to the world again.

The happier life—not found among the streets
Where broken lives and other men's defeats
Blow with the litter that encamps like squatters
Up sheltered alleys in old business quarters;
And just as seldom found in rural shires
Of bumptious villagers or dreaming spires.
The happy life is dreamt, just like the love
Before the first, and is not quite enough.
Insufficient perfections—what else is there?
Immaculate, unbothered lives, like air
Or glass, stray round us, better selves, unshadows
Doing different though they wear our clothes.
I only live like mine at café tables
Waiting for a friend, when the impossibles
Invent my future; or when feeling good
Drink five draught sherries from the wood;
Or drowse with a Havana and the cat;
Or please my wife with dinner and a hat;
Or watch half-sleeping from the rhythmic train
Long summer distance on the mellow plain,
So right, I am as minerals or rain.

Five Years Married

We have been waltzing in the foggy meadows
At the edges of cliffs, in outmoded evening dress.
Our lives are out of date, both truly obsolete.
Years ago, I dreamt I would write this poem.
I recognize the meadows, that exact view of the sea,
And the hand in my hand, familiar with rings,
The veins in the right places, a tiny flaw on the skin,
Your hand, and my hand, and your face that I cannot see.

Runners

Your skin is whiter, and as you bend fat tells
Your eight years of less than Spartan marriage.
Any man can see what you have been, your legs
That too much sitting cannot discompose,
And synthesis of all movement, your running.
Men still remember you, on the last lap
Of your favourite distance, commander of championships.

Today through the hilly wood, we knew only
Lack of ease, the detritus of beauty
Left to athletes who betray their rule,
A longing of mind for its body, in which
There is no pride, or applause, and whisky
Comes back through months working against us,
The woods are smoke-filled rooms, but no one dare stop.

The Philologists

Familiar with you, for I have studied your life
Like the dead languages we understand but cannot speak,
There is no need for us to talk. We know all that
Conversational stuff, pleasantries, common things.
It is silence we love, and the mind asleep
In the room it goes to after work, the flowers there
Withered, their broken parts in the dust of the tabletop,
The yellow newspapers, empty inkbottles, and books
In the two high bookcases with glass doors that lock.

After the War

The soldiers came, brewed tea in Snoddy's field
Beside the wood from where we watched them pee
In Snoddy's stagnant pond, small boys hidden
In pines and firs. The soldiers stood or sat
Ten minutes in the field, some officers apart
With the select problems of a map. Before,
Soldiers were imagined, we were them, gunfire
In our mouths, most cunning local skirmishers.
Their sudden arrival silenced us. I lay down
On the grass and saw the blue shards of an egg
We'd broken, its warm yolk on the green grass,
And pine cones like little hand grenades.

One burst from an imaginary Browning,
A grenade well thrown by a child's arm,
And all these faces like our fathers' faces
Would fall back bleeding, trucks would burst in flames,
A blood-stained map would float on Snoddy's pond.
Our ambush made the soldiers laugh, and some
Made booming noises from behind real rifles
As we ran among them begging for badges,
Our plimsolls on the fallen May-blossom
Like boots on the faces of dead children.
But one of us had left. I saw him go
Out through the gate, I heard him on the road
Running to his mother's house. They lived alone,
Behind a hedge round an untended garden
Filled with broken toys, abrasive loss;
A swing that creaked, a rusted bicycle.
He went inside just as the convoy passed.

D

Alternative

The silence in a prodigal's purse,
The flower when the bee's left it;
The world that might be given us
Should this world fail.

Modern Love

It is summer, and we are in a house
That is not ours, sitting at a table
Enjoying minutes of a rented silence,
The upstairs people gone. The pigeons lull
To sleep the under-tens and invalids,
The tree shakes out its shadows to the grass,
The roses rove through the wilds of my neglect.
Our lives flap, and we have no hope of better
happiness than this, not much to show for love
But how we are, or how this evening is,
Unpeopled, silent, and where we are alive
In a domestic love, seemingly alone,
All other lives worn down to trees and sunlight,
Looking forward to a visit from the cat.

Guerrillas

They lived on farms, were stout and freckled, knew
Our country differently, from work, not play.
Fathers or brothers brought them to school in cars,
Dung on the doors, fresh eggs in the back.
The teachers favoured them for their wealth,
Daffodils and free eggs, and we envied them
The ownership of all the land we roved on,
Their dangerous dogs and stately horses,
The fruit we had to steal, their land being
Income, and ours a mysterious provider.
They owned the shadows cast by every branch,
Chestnuts and flowers, water, the awkward wire.
Their sullen eyes demanded rent, and so
We shouted the bad words to their sisters,
Threw stones at hens, blocked up the froggy drains.
Outlaws from dark woods and quarries,
We plundered all we envied and had not got,
As if the disinherited from farther back
Came to our blood like a knife to a hand.

Under the Stone

They sleep out the day in Grimsby, Goole, or Hull,
The sleep of Empire sherry and unspeakable liquors,
And clumsily beg at the Saturday cinema queues
From steady workers and their penny-pinching girlfriends,
The washed and sober, who only want to laugh or listen.

These men remind them of the back of their minds.
Splendid barbarians, they form tribes in the slums
Up certain dim streets, the tribes of second-hand,
In empty houses no one wants to buy,
Abandoned rooms the poor have given up.

No one wants to see them, in a grey dawn, walk down
The empty streets, an army of unkept appointments,
Broken promises, as drab as fog,
Like portents meaning bad harvests, unemployment,
Cavalry in the streets, and children shouting 'Bread! Bread!'

But they mean nothing, they live under the stone.
They are their own failures and our nightmares
Or longings for squalor, the bad meanings we are.
They like it like that. It makes them happy,
Walking the rubble fields where once houses were.

The New Girls

The dancing and drinking go on into the night
In the rooms of Edwardian houses,
In flats that cads and fashionable young couples rent,
Where the parties of Saturday happen
After the pub everyone goes to has closed.

There are always the girls there no one's seen before,
Who soon become known and their first names remembered.
Replacing the girls who 'simply just vanished'
To new jobs in London or husbands who've quietened down.
The new girls leave with the men who brought them

To rooms nearby in the same district, or one just like it.
At dawn, three streets from their homes,
The girls leave cars with doors that slam,
Engines that sound like men's contemptuous laughter,
As they disappear at fifty down an empty street.

Then they reach the door, and turn the key, and know
They have been listening to their own footsteps
In the silence of Sunday before the milkmen,
When the cats are coming home to eat, and water dripping
From the bridge is heard a hundred yards away.

Saturday Night Function

The cinemas empty, and backs of seats
Become varnished waves, the light ordinary.

Solemn couples go through the coat routine,
Check for gloves, cigarette case, spectacles.

First out, the fat boys glide to their doorways
To eat double fish and chips and watch the thin.

Ushers lead out the sleepy old men.
The happy couples are already miles away.

Seducers, anxious for this week's insert,
Their hands warming in shiny black gloves,

Have hailed black patent leather taxis
And taken the girl to a flat in the suburbs.

The other style are out in the country,
Love among the spanners in ample vans.

Bored narcissists, for whom friendship is an ache,
Look for themselves in bus-queues and railway stations.

The stylish youths speed to parties
Intent on any wildness that doesn't make you fat

And you don't have to pay for. Lonely drunks
Collide with the respectable, begging their pardons.

In the city rhythm of the last bus home
Is where I come in, imagining the night

Of four hundred thousand lives,
A man bleeding after a brawl,

A child with toothache after too much cake.
Night after night, the same sleep, machines,

Wheels, lights, still alive when the lives rest,
The silence after entertainment.

A Faber Melancholy

(For P. L. and I. H.)

These days my discontents surpass
All the freedoms laws have left me with.
I live beneath a tree, I sleep on grass,
And think too much about the ways of death.
    Here nothing reaches me except a few bills,
    Letters from friends and a book from Blackwell's.

Morose, and scared, I am outside
In cities other people would avoid,
A deckchair journalist, who swallows pride
With quantities of doleful lines, employed
    To grow his own lettuce, live off berries
    At the end of routes, other side of ferries.

No time, no time, no meditation.
There are gradual but disastrous happenings
That prevent language. They turn me on;
They turn me *off*. They really make things
    Like being alive difficult. It's awful.
    Mr. Say-Nothing, my tongue is a bottle.

And in a garden, over fences,
A toy soprano sings *bel canto* airs.
If I shut my eyes I will hear silences
And the greenfly breathing in my hair.
    How did this happen? They thought I was shy
    Or evil, but I turned out to be a spy

Among the foxgloves—Chance garlands
Poets, and classical-shaped leaves make light

Crowded for the rose, so many flimsy strands
That weave a strangeness. Now, out of sight,
  Submerged in shadows where the leaves are pale,
  Through stillnesses malicious tendrils trail,

Like careers, a blemished progress
On a stale, romantic earth. There is dirt
Under my fingernails, a sprinkled mess
Of soot and insects trembles on my shirt.
  Here forever, I'd see the wonders break,
  The reputations and the roses flake.

A thorn has scored my writing hand.
No one now can have Byron's love, or fry
With Shelley in great company on the sand.
To do is only to be like, or try,
  And to achieve is only to be less
  Than all these dead. There is no success.

Over the pavements of microgroove
With *mobile vulgus*, the popular
Arrive with praise and protest, and they move
So accurately, like the latest film star.
  Switch on the wireless, listen to The Pips,
  Go tell it to the Ministry of Paperclips.

I think I'm Horace with a view
Of the gasworks. Augustus, you are not
In this city tonight. You're not, are you?
We knew it had to change, the wonders rot.
  No world of fixities. Crude motion rocks
  The world's foundations to its very socks.

Too much Mozart, and too much Pope.
Now we have the era of reputations,

A land of budgie hotels, the downhill slope
To a thousand abandoned railway stations.
    They water-ski in what were gravel pits,
    And men in boiler suits crowd out the Ritz.

A spray of summer rain releases
Many smells. It stops. And then the butterflies
Emerge from freshened hides, the white pieces
That cruise like openings of startled eyes
    Over the sliding grass, and watch from walls
    Thick wasps imbibing death from sodden windfalls.

Philip and Ian, we haven't much
In common but serious will and an imprint;
Frail fellowship no century can touch
Or life in Sump City make less confident;
    Three writers writing for the under-read
    And risk all privacies to make life said.

Tennysonian or Hardyesque,
To find authentic hurt and what will move
All poets labour inward at a desk.
If they find wisdom, it's that art and love
Survive behind the times to keep us sane.
And knowing that, there's nothing to complain
Or rail about. For nothing could improve,
No matter the love you had, or what you'd risk.
    Then keep us safe, so that these times will slide
    Safe to survival, and find the freshened hide.

Up in Duggie's Room

Your room repels, too many cats, the bed
Unmade beneath the garret skylight,
Possessions chosen too much for effect;
Your young man's alto saxophone, select
Books your conversation shows you've read,
A fancy pan to puke in when you're tight.

But this is where you live, and you're my friend.
Whatever we think bonds us would not fix
Itself to objects only I would recommend
To ownership. No visible appearance
Tells it to others, no style or pretence
Pinned like your unbeliever's crucifix
Above your bed, your faded Indian rug
And sad chaise-longue, the antique dealer's mug.

Though so much different in the way we live
We share a feeling for the genuine excess,
Each life a beautiful alternative,
Both equally profane, your happiness
In reaching for abundance with a style
That makes me be my age and makes me smile,

While I grow fat and dull, the saddest wit,
Hard in the head but softer in the tit,
Who was the once exuberantly brute.
The shams of youth and young man's privilege,
The mornings when you wake up in a hedge
And walk home singing in a haggard suit—
They form the wasted days, that treacherous silt,

That to remember truly takes the piss
As much as alcohol or cannabis,
And that to sink in tells you how I've felt
Watching you reach the first elusive clue,
To learn, like me, that there is nothing new.

Bird Poet

Touring the resorts
Like a hotel inspector,
Each one has its meals
And headaches and wonder.
You are not yet mad,
But something is happening.
The coast is lively.
Thalassian tourists
Agog at sea-scenery
Drink tea in cars;
Glass and chrome fittings
Flash random signals
Of uselessness over
What men cannot make:
Lives of water, the sea
Nursing disaster,
Sunk salty objects.
Western landladies
On Largs promenade
Are talking of grocers,
The high cost of funerals.
Four sunny sportsmen
And four sullen wives
Play obstacle golf.
A girl with a headache
Goes to bed early.
The man with a headache
Leaves the hotel,
Looks through the windows
Of the empty ballroom,

Listens to knives and forks,
Children and fruit-machines.
Fly away Douglas,
You don't really like this.
Sit on a rock
And make white marks,
Snatch somebody's bun.
Fly over the town
To the hotel on the hill,
Sit by the window,
Watch the girl sleeping,
Stand on the table
Beside her white face,
Watch the wool gather
On the glass of water;
Watch all get dark
And the light slip under
The door like a letter,
A secret that goes
Before you can touch it.
Stand on the table
Beside her head,
The girl with the headache,
The glass and the seagull;
Inside your love
Are gods and stories,
Metamorphoses, escapes.
Tomorrow another hotel
Will encounter you,
You will dine from its plates,
You will sit by the girl
And nothing will change.

Fixed

The world is at its weediest
And putting gardeners to the test;
My favourite butterflies flap through
The drifting wool of willow-herb
And thorns of the wild roses barb
Some tiny corners of the view.
From lily-can to honey-byke
Bees take their precious loads across,
While in the shadows of the dyke
The warm damps utter moss.
  Young gardens of the bungalows
That nurture lettuces and rose
Now own these fields, and the hollows
Where the bramble-brake and fern
Shimmering at noon would earn
The greenest share of light, now fill
With road and lamp-post, window-sill,
Gate and garage. Lawnmowing dusks
And the fatherly processions
Vibrate a thousand small possessions,
The rattle in a pram, a jar
With marbles, bottles in a bar.
But here once harvest-emptied husks
Drifted over golden fields. There,
In that grain-dismembered air,
Children watched sail past tall cranes
Prime ships set for the shipping lanes.
  On that southern, pastoral side
Of the tall, shipyarded Clyde,
The merchant's sump, once children hid

In a wheat-and-orchard parish
That satisfied each muted wish,
And through their minds the parish slid.
   Under the wooded hill, the dead
Fitz-alan took from Somerled
With local levies, a hiding child
Once sensed behind him; or the wild
Votadini; and Strathclyde's king
Listening to his minstrel sing;
While there a troop of Roman horse
Was tethered to the birch and gorse;
And here, too, John, ninth of Argyle,
Was captured in the rain, that guile
Might get its own back on the Campbells,
Ambushed in the ferns and brambles;
And gentlemen from Bar and Park
Once suddenly appeared, to stare
At finding sleeping urchins there
So strangely dressed. Their sheep-dogs barked,
And the waking children, frightened,
Could not know they'd been enlightened
By 1800 being shown
New times on land it used to own.
These two friends dressed like Scott or Burns
Turned back through the trees and ferns
And wisely laughed. So out of time,
No watches tick and no clocks chime,
But only the barking of a dog
Along the river in the river-fog.
And only children now believe
St. Conval sailed here on a stone
To found his church. Faith of their own,
Legends in the shadow of the town
Defy alternatives, survive
Shipyards and jets. Fox and frog,

Magpie and plover, they seem to sense
That they inherit every tense.
Underneath what's left of what's left
That hides the snake and soggy eft,
The ruins of our footprints slide
Beneath waves of a silent tide.

   In all its clay and wooden parts,
A perfect place. For love of them,
I make into a local emblem
Mud and moss-padded banks of Carts;
The summer light on white-washed byre
And sticklebacks in all the burns
And bulbous water over stones;
The horses that the rich girl owns
Longed for by boys in Renfrewshire;
Grim driftwood that the Clyde returns
To fill the festering lagoons;
Each modest hill, and sticky blaze
Of rhododendron-coloured days
Smouldering in the afternoons.
   Rivers seem smaller now, and glades
More miniature by several shades.
I should have known. For look, how big
My hands are now, those urchins' paws
That took the tall headmaster's tawse.
How big my hands; and short the rigg.
And I did not hear the laughter
In the dust that once rose after
Plough-horses on the lanes; and the smell
Of that treasured redolence,
Cut hay, did not attract at all.
Only disappointment made much sense,
As if I had come back to try
To wear the fabric of a lie,

To be a child, or re-invent
All that that childhood had not meant.
    Yet there is rightness in my lies,
Visited unfactual landscape of
The inner silences of love,
These parks and trees behind the eyes:
The certain fields through which must wade
That certain bride my life has made,
The fair grass tall on gentle hills
Down which unhurried water spills
Its tender humps, and where I know
The place where better berries grow;
The place where happiness is set
And all renewing loves are met,
By ivied walls or by the river
When at dusk the world's a park;
And though I change, and sunlight's never
The same again, or woods so dark,
And active generations cry, 'Forget, Forget!'
These are the fields of love and death,
And cannot change, were meant to be
Forever there distortedly,
The fixed and visionary part of me.

Spoken to by Six

(for three voices:
the hags', a nun-doctor who asked one question, and mine)

Now we are six, *say the years*,
Now it is just six of us
Since the violent swerve, the crash,

The fool we sent to overtake you.
Was it exciting? a thrill?
The man behind you said, 'Boy oh boy!' and he'd seen
   nothing like it.

Now we are six,
It is six years since you took
The snapshot at Niagara three hours before

Smiling in a row of three
At the edge of the blue, roaring lament
For the lost minerals of the continent.

There are six of us.
Six. Do you know what that means?
It means you haven't forgotten.

Have you? The glass, the blood,
The fish-like eyes of the curious
And the way the cops laughed.

You thought their cap badges
Were like little birds. You idiot,
You must have been disturbed.

68

Not to mention the light motorcycles
And the girls with transistors.
A nice touch, that. Coincidence did well.

Oh my dear, was she one in a million?
Listen to us laughing! The death ha-ha.
She *was* one in a million,

And we are six out of millions.
People live in us and have nasty shocks.
We are just your friendly neighbourhood gap.

It was just too bad, a nice girl like that
With such a clever husband, and the future.
Our future, of course. Us. The same Corporation.

Death alive, the ever-expanding hags, your memory.
We're tough. Our big book says your flesh is as grass.
So try tying that up with the death-bandage.

Route 90, oh dusty sump,
Close to the vineyards,
I am still hopelessly mixed up;

Erie was so hot, and a stray dog
Barked at the door of the Casualty Department.
You stare death in the face, and catch it
With your teeth, like a bullet. Sleight of soul.

'Is she a Catholic?'
Baptize the foetus,
Get the priest, get the President, get God.

Now don't you fret honey, and don't complain.
Just sentimentalize the pain.

And don't you forget, all you out there,
Don't you forget
The Six, the Seven, the Eight . . .

The Hour

Grey garden, tree-slag
At four o'clock,

The Sylvia Plath hour.
The daisies are like frost,

Deaths of many babies;
And daisies under dew,

Many unbirths in the frog-morning.
No shining is possible,

It is grey as matter,
Grey as tennis shoes.

It is grey-grey,
The opposite colour of whisky.

There is no sky at four o'clock,
Only light that oozes grudgingly

Ivy dark as guilt,
Hardware of the dawn;

Inert outline of trees,
A lighted window, slabs of wall,

Lifeless individuality,
Like saliva, like self-knowledge.

There is no world beyond that:
No absorbing frivolity,

No newspapers with columns
On how to know the best wines,

No cross-Channel ferries,
No banks and no bookshops.

You might say it is just negative,
Or free, a long-division sum forever.

Four o'clock, you blank,
I might even get to like you.

Will I see you often,
Your roomless world of headaches,

Stiffly vegetable?
You chirp like old doors opened,

You detach in surprising black birds.
Will you do something for me?

Don't be like the rest of the summer.
Summer's a sentimental mess,

Like being young.
And don't visit me; stay outside.

Keep me watching you.
Keep me cold. Keep me alive. Keep me.